Dedication

To the leaders who carry the weight of responsibility beyond
the project plan.

MAXMETRICS® PROJECT LEADERSHIP SERIES

Responsible Project Leadership

in the Age of

Digital Accountability

A Practical Guide to Agile Delivery and Ethical Leadership

GLORIA J. MILLER, DBA

ATLANTA | HEIDELBERG

Responsible Project Leadership in the Age of Digital Accountability

Library of Congress Control Number: 2026906238

International Standard Book Number:

979-8-9952095-0-8 Paperback United States

979-8-9952095-1-5 Paperback Europe

979-8-9952095-2-2 ePub

979-8-9952095-3-9 Kindle

Preface

In 2020, I published the third edition of *Going Agile Project Management Practices*.

This book is the result of more than three decades of experience in information and communication technology, as well as my belief—formed as early as the late 1990s that projects must be iterative and incremental. I observed plan-driven projects struggle under uncertainty and learned through both success and failure that adaptability is essential.

At that time, the primary challenge organizations faced was transitioning from traditional project management to agile methodologies. The focus was on flexibility, timeboxing, collaboration, and integrating agile practices into structured project environments.

Then the world began to accelerate.

Cloud platforms have become the default operating environment. Digital ecosystems have replaced isolated systems. Artificial intelligence has transitioned from experimentation to operational deployment. Regulators have increased scrutiny. Societal expectations have shifted. Data has become both an asset and a liability.

Projects were no longer solely focused on delivering working software quickly.

They focused on deploying systems that learn, influence decisions, scale globally, and persist long after the project team has disbanded.

Agility remained essential.

However, agility alone was no longer sufficient.

In the years since *Going Agile*, I have led and revitalized complex AI and cloud-based transformations across banking, insurance, retail, manufacturing, and government sectors. I have witnessed organizations deliver innovative digital solutions, and I have also observed them face regulatory investigations, ethical scrutiny, uncontrolled cloud spending, and stakeholder backlash.

The common thread in both success and failure was not the methodology.

It was governance.

It was accountability.

It was a clear sense of responsibility.

It depended on whether leaders escalated issues early or allowed them to linger.

It was about whether data was traceable, whether decisions were documented, and whether sponsors truly understood what they were approving.

The question was whether ethical considerations were embedded from the start or treated as an afterthought.

This book reflects that evolution.

It builds upon the foundation of agile thinking presented in *Going Agile*, but extends it into a broader, more integrated leadership model. This model incorporates recognized global standards, performance domain thinking, and practical field experience. Additionally, it introduces two critical domains essential for complex digital or AI environments: Ethics Management and Digital Asset and Record Governance.

Artificial intelligence, in particular, changes the stakes.

AI systems can influence financial approvals, employment decisions, credit risk scoring, healthcare recommendations, and regulatory compliance. However, AI itself is not accountable; people are.

The further we advance toward automation and autonomy, the more disciplined governance must become.

Over the course of my career—including research in AI accountability and project governance, as well as recognition within the IEEE community—I have come to view project management not merely as a delivery discipline but as a system of structured responsibility.

Projects are temporary organizations.

Their consequences are not inevitable.

This book presents the Governance, Responsibility, Integrity, and Performance Framework (GRIP Framework) as a practical integration of governance, agility, ethics, stakeholder accountability, structured digital asset and record management, and AI oversight. It does not reject agile principles; rather, it represents their maturation.

Agility enhances speed.

Governance fosters trust.

Ethics enables legitimacy.

Digital asset governance ensures defensibility.

Leadership integrates all of them.

If *Going Agile* is about adapting to change, this book focuses on managing change responsibly in an AI-driven world.

My philosophy remains simple:

Do the right thing as early as possible.

Escalate risks before they develop into crises. Structure communication clearly. Ensure that the people performing the work establish realistic commitments. Protect those who may be affected, even if they are not present in the room. Document decisions thoroughly so they can be justified later.

Modern project management is no longer solely focused on delivering results.

It is about delivering results that earn trust.

I hope this book helps you achieve exactly that.

Gloria J. Miller, DBA

Contents

I Foundations of Responsible Project Leadership

III   Governance, Stakeholders, and Integration

IV Closing and References

List of Figures

List of Tables

How to Use This Book

This book is designed as a practical guide to leadership.

It can be read from beginning to end to fully understand the structure of responsible project leadership. It can also be used selectively, depending on your experience level and the challenges you face.

1. If You Are New to Modern Project Leadership

Begin with the foundational chapters.

These chapters build the conceptual model that supports everything that follows. They introduce the language and structure of the **Governance, Responsibility, Integrity, and Performance Framework**.

Once this foundation is clear, the later chapters become easier to apply in practice.

2. If You Need Help With a Project Right Now

Use this book as a structured diagnostic tool.

Before reacting to symptoms, identify which performance domain is under stress:

- Unclear decision-making authority or escalation confusion usually signals a governance weakness.

- Resistance, misalignment, or slow approvals often indicate stakeholder issues.

- Tool sprawl, cloud cost growth, or documentation gaps point to digital environment weaknesses.

- AI-related issues such as opacity, bias exposure, and accountability concerns require strengthened AI governance and ethical controls.

- If multiple areas are unstable, revisit the integration chapter to restore structural alignment.

After identifying the stress point, apply the tools, tables, and reflection questions provided in that section.

3. Distinguishing Between Using AI and Managing AI

This book distinguishes between two different realities:

- Using AI to improve project planning, reporting, forecasting, and knowledge management.

- Managing a project that involves building or deploying an AI system.

The first method improves efficiency. The second requires heightened governance, ethical oversight, and structured accountability.

Apply the appropriate guidance according to your situation.

4. Use the Tools in Governance Settings

The checklists, responsibility mappings, stakeholder frameworks, and domain tables are designed for practical use. They are intended to support disciplined conversation, not to create bureaucracy.

5. Think in Systems, Not Silos

Each performance domain is presented separately for clarity; however, in practice, they operate as an integrated system.

When governance weakens, stakeholder trust declines. When digital asset and record management fail, accountability weakens. When ethical guardrails are ignored, both reputational and regulatory risks increase.

Use this book not as a checklist of isolated controls but as a guide for structured, responsible integration across the Governance, Responsibility, Integrity, and Performance Framework.

Introduction

Project management is continuously evolving.

For decades, success was measured by scope, schedule, and cost. Projects were evaluated based on their ability to deliver defined outputs within agreed-upon constraints.

Today, that definition is no longer sufficient.

Modern projects operate in an era defined by digital accountability. They are built on cloud platforms, shaped by regulatory scrutiny, and increasingly influenced by artificial intelligence. They generate data on a large scale, leave permanent digital traces, and affect individuals and communities far beyond the original business case.

In this environment, performance is clearly visible. Decisions have been recorded. The consequences extend beyond the project team.

Expectations have changed.

Organizations are expected not only to deliver efficiently but also to deliver responsibly. They must protect data, demonstrate transparency, manage ethical risks, and preserve stakeholder trust.

Project leadership cannot remain static; it must integrate agility with structure, innovation with oversight, and value creation with accountability.

This book presents a practical approach to responsible project leadership. It builds upon recognized global standards and proven delivery practices, including:

- Structured governance and lifecycle management

- Principle-based performance domains

- Agile and hybrid delivery models

- Cloud and digital operating environments

- Artificial intelligence applications in projects

At the same time, it extends traditional practice by formally integrating two critical domains:

- Ethics Management

- Digital Asset and Record Governance

These are mandatory enhancements. They are structural requirements for delivering value in environments where decisions must be explainable, traceable, and defensible.

Throughout this book, these elements are integrated into the Governance, Responsibility, Integrity, and Performance Framework^{TM}—a practical model designed to help leaders deliver with clarity, discipline, and integrity.

This is not a theoretical text.

It is written for project managers, sponsors, executives, and governance professionals working in environments where:

- Requirements evolve rapidly.

- Regulatory exposure is a real concern.

- Data must be auditable.

- AI systems influence outcomes.

- Trust determines long-term success.

Modern project management is no longer just about delivering outputs. It is about delivering value responsibly.

This book is intended for environments where regulatory exposure, AI systems, and digital traceability render traditional project management methods inadequate.

Before exploring each domain in detail, it is helpful to view the integrated structure at a glance.

The Governance, Responsibility, Integrity, and Performance Framework: An Overview

Modern projects operate in environments defined by:

- Regulatory exposure

- Artificial intelligence systems

- Cloud-based infrastructure

- Permanent digital traceability

- Expanding stakeholder impact

Traditional project management disciplines remain necessary. They are no longer sufficient.

The Governance, Responsibility, Integrity, and Performance Framework integrates ten interdependent performance domains into a unified governance system.

Core Design Logic

- **Governance at the Core** Defines authority, escalation procedures, accountability, and oversight mechanisms.

- **Ethics as a Normative Boundary** Ensures that value creation does not cause harm.

- **Digital Asset and Record Governance as Transparency Backbone** Enables traceability, audit readiness, and defensibility.

- **Stakeholders as a Legitimacy Interface** Protects trust and manages impact effectively.

- **Operational Domains as the Execution Engine** Scope, schedule, financials, risk, resources, and quality translate strategy into delivery.

These domains do not operate independently.

- Governance stabilizes the system.

- Ethics constrain risk-taking.

- Digital asset governance preserves accountability.

- Stakeholder engagement protects legitimacy.

- Operational domains execute within clearly defined boundaries.

When one domain weakens, the entire system becomes destabilized. When the domains are integrated, resilience improves.

This book explains how to design, govern, and lead projects using an integrated model.

Part I

Foundations of Responsible Project Leadership

Chapter 1

What Is a Modern Project?

A project is a temporary effort undertaken to create a unique product, service, or result.

Projects serve as the primary vehicles of change within organizations. They introduce new systems, transform operations, launch digital platforms, and implement innovations.

Every project has a defined beginning and end. It operates with structured objectives, allocated resources, and measurable outcomes.

However, modern projects operate in fundamentally different environments than those of the past. In this book, "modern" does not refer to recency alone. Instead, it refers to projects delivered within digitally traceable, cloud-based, AI-influenced, and highly regulated ecosystems.

They exist within digital ecosystems where technology is not simply a tool but the operating environment itself. In these settings, decisions are preserved as data, systems scale globally by default, and accountability extends beyond the project team.

1.1 How Modern Projects Structurally Differ

Traditional projects were often characterized by the following features:

- Clearly defined requirements at the initiation phase

- Linear, predictive life cycles

- Stable technological infrastructures

- Limited regulatory scrutiny

- Narrow stakeholder impact

Modern projects operate under different conditions.
They:

- use agile or hybrid life cycles to effectively respond to change

- depend on cloud services and shared platforms

- rely on distributed digital collaboration

- generate large volumes of both structured and unstructured data

- frequently incorporate artificial intelligence

- operate under heightened regulatory oversight

- must consider ethical and societal consequences

The distinction is not incremental; it is structural. Traditional project management assumed bounded systems, limited traceability, and localized impact. Conversely, modern projects operate within persistent digital ecosystems where decisions, data, and consequences extend far beyond project closure.

These characteristics increase both opportunity and complexity.

1.2   Technology as an Operating Environment

In many industries, technology is no longer just a supporting function; it has become the primary operating environment.

Cloud platforms allow rapid scaling and global deployment.

Digital collaboration tools enable distributed teams to work together in real time.

Data systems continuously capture user behavior, operational metrics, and performance signals.

Artificial intelligence systems can influence decisions, automate tasks, or generate outputs autonomously.

This technological integration means that projects today:

- Move faster

- Affect more stakeholders

- Leave digital evidence trails

- Create long-term dependencies

The consequences of project decisions are significantly amplified.

1.3 Expanded Accountability

Modern projects must operate within expanded accountability expectations shaped by digital traceability and regulatory oversight.

Organizations are expected to:

- Protect personal data

- Demonstrate transparency

- Prevent bias and discrimination

- Ensure system security

- Comply with international standards and regulations

Projects now affect more than just internal operations.

They may influence customers, communities, regulators, and society as a whole.

This expands the responsibilities of project leadership beyond delivery to include governance, defensibility, and stewardship of long-term impact.

Why This Matters

Organizations no longer compete solely based on cost and schedule.

They compete on:

- Speed of innovation

- Ability to adapt

- Quality of digital experience

- Trust and credibility

- Responsible technology use

In digitally accountable environments, trust functions as strategic capital. A project that delivers quickly but undermines trust causes long-term damage.

Poorly managed digital or AI initiatives can result in:

- Regulatory fines

- Legal exposure

- Data breaches

- Reputational damage

- Loss of stakeholder confidence

Conversely, organizations that integrate structured governance, ethical oversight, strong digital asset and record management, and active stakeholder engagement into their projects gain a competitive advantage.

They deliver innovation responsibly.

1.4   The Leadership Shift

Because modern projects operate within complex digital ecosystems, project leaders must shift from task coordination to systems leadership.

They must:

- Balance agility with governance

- Integrate ethics into decision-making

- Ensure accountability in AI systems

- Manage data as a strategic asset

- Protect stakeholder trust

A modern project is defined not only by the technology it employs. It is defined by the level of traceability, regulatory exposure, AI influence, stakeholder reach, and governance intensity embedded within its operating environment.

It is defined by the responsibility with which it is delivered.

Understanding this structural shift forms the foundation for everything that follows in this book. The Governance, Responsibility, Integrity, and Performance Framework is designed as a structured response to this modern operating reality.

Chapter 2

Standards That Guide Modern Projects

Project management is a global profession; however, most organizations do not execute projects by strictly adhering to a single standard.

In practice, leaders adopt strategies that are effective:

- a governance structure that aligns with decision speed and risk,

- a lifecycle approach that matches uncertainty,

- and a common language that keeps sponsors, teams, and auditors aligned.

Standards are important because they reduce improvisation. They help you deliver with discipline *without* creating bureaucracy.

2.1 Major Project Standards and Their Uses

There is no single global standard that every organization follows. Instead, most environments draw from a limited set of widely recognized frameworks.

The point is not to memorize them. The goal is to understand the strengths of each standard and how to apply them pragmatically.

2.1.1 ISO 21502 Guidance

International Organization for Standardization (ISO) 21502 *Guidance on Project Management* is especially helpful when clarity and consistency are needed across teams, countries, or business units (International Standards Organization, 2020).

Use ISO thinking when:

- governance roles must be explicit,

- sponsor accountability must be visible,

- lifecycle activities must be structured,

- and project work must align with the organizational strategy.

A practical ISO reminder is that projects exist to realize benefits, not just to produce deliverables.

2.1.2　PMI PMBOK® Guide

The Project Management Institute (PMI) *Project Management Body of Knowledge (PMBOK®) Guide* is useful when you need a performance-focused view of project success (Project Management Institute, 2025).

It is most effective when your organization aims to move beyond checklist delivery and asks:

- Are we delivering value?

- Are we managing the system as a whole, rather than just individual tasks?

- Are we improving decision quality across various domains?

A core PMBOK message is that success includes both:

- efficiency (on time, on budget), and

- effectiveness (value delivered and outcomes achieved).

2.1.3　APM Body of Knowledge

Association for Project Management (APM) is useful when a stronger emphasis on professional judgment, leadership maturity, and project complexity is desired (Association for Project Management, 2019).

APM thinking is helpful when:

- sponsorship and governance must be strengthened,

- behavioral capability influences outcomes,

- sustainability expectations matter,

- and complexity is not purely technical.

It reinforces an important reality: competence is not only technical but also behavioral and ethical.

2.1.4 PRINCE2

PRINCE2 is useful when projects require formal control, documentation discipline, and stage-based decision points (The Stationery Office, 2017).

It fits well when:

- roles must be clearly assigned,

- the business case must be consistently defended throughout,

- stage approvals are required,

- and management products must be consistent.

PRINCE2s practical strength lies in its principle of continued business justification: if the project no longer delivers value, it must be changed or terminated.

2.2 What These Standards Have in Common

Despite differences in terminology, the shared foundations are consistent.

Across ISO, PMI, APM, and PRINCE2 standards:

- projects must align with the strategy,

- governance and accountability must be explicit,

- risks must be actively managed,

- stakeholders must be engaged,

- and value delivery defines success.

This is why most organizations blend various standards. They are not simply choosing a brand; they are building a functional operating model.

2.3 Where Standards Alone Are Not Enough

Many standards were designed before todays delivery realities became the norm:

- cloud-based infrastructure and outsourced platforms,

- agile delivery at enterprise scale,

- AI systems with probabilistic outcomes,

- regulated data governance expectations,

- and increased public demand for ethical accountability.

The standards remain relevant; however, accountable projects require more deliberate integration across:

- governance structures and decision rights,

- agile and hybrid delivery,

- vendor and platform management,

- ethical oversight,

- and digital asset and record governance.

If these elements are not integrated, projects do not fail due to a lack of effort from the teams. They fail because the control systems do not match the environment.

2.4   How This Book Integrates Standards

The framework presented in this book draws on the strongest elements of established standards and directs them toward practical implementation.

It emphasizes:

- governance clarity and sponsor visibility,

- value-driven success measurement,

- lifecycle discipline and tailoring,

- risk escalation and accountability,

- and stakeholder legitimacy and trust.

It also extends traditional approaches by explicitly addressing two domains within complex digital and AI delivery environments:

- Ethics Management

- Digital Asset and Record Governance

These are not optional add-ons. There are structural requirements when projects operate within digital and AI-driven ecosystems.

2.5 Why This Integrated Model Matters

Projects today must deliver value quickly while maintaining defensibility.

That means leaders must be able to:

- move quickly without losing control,

- demonstrate compliance without creating paralysis,

- protect stakeholder trust under scrutiny,

- and sustain governance after go-live.

The next chapter introduces the unified structure of **project management performance domains**. This structure synthesizes proven principles from major standards and adapts them to address the realities of cloud computing, data management, and AI-enabled delivery.

It is not a new theory. It is a disciplined integration process designed for real project environments.

Chapter 3

Project Management Performance Domains

Projects do not fail because leaders forget terminology.

They fail simply when critical areas of responsibility remain unmanaged.

This book uses the term **project management performance domain** to describe the major areas that must be actively managed throughout the project lifecycle. The terminology aligns with the PMI *PMBOK® Guide* and is further integrated with concepts and practices from ISO, APM, PRINCE2, and contemporary governance research (Miller, 2025a).

A performance domain is not a checklist.

It is a leadership obligation.

Each domain represents a cluster of decisions, controls, and behaviors that shape whether a project delivers value in a responsible and sustainable manner.

The question is not:

> Do we know these domains?

The question is:

> Are we actively governing them?

3.1 The Core Performance Domains in Practice

The traditional domains remain essential. The changes in complex digital and AI environments are not about their relevance; rather, it is the intensity with which they must be managed.

3.1.1 Governance Performance Domain

Use the governance domain to answer:

> Who decides, on what basis, and what is the escalation path?

Governance aligns the project with the overall strategy, defines decision-making authority, and clarifies when issues must be escalated.

If governance is weak:

- scope drifts,

- risk escalates silently,

- accountability becomes unclear.

Strong governance does not delay projects. It prevents confusion and protects legitimacy.

This domain introduces governance as an operational responsibility throughout the lifecycle. A deeper examination of governance structures, escalation design, and accountability frameworks is provided in Chapter 9.

3.1.2 Scope Performance Domain

The scope of a discipline defines its boundaries.

Use this domain when:

- requirements expand quickly,

- stakeholders request additional features,

- innovation pressures challenge clarity,

- or system behavior may have ethical or societal implications.

Scope encompasses more than just a list of deliverables. It is a shared contract among the sponsor, the project manager, and the organization that defines what the system is intended to do, and what it is not intended to do.

A well-defined scope document:

- clarifies expected system behavior,

- aligns the project to strategic objectives,

- anticipates potential misuse or unintended consequences

- and establishes defensible boundaries for accountability.

In AI projects, the scope should explicitly address:

- intended beneficiaries,

- foreseeable societal impacts,

- and guardrails that prevent harm.

Scope protects focus.

Without it, projects consume resources without delivering proportional value or introducing risks beyond their original scope.

3.1.3 Schedule Performance Domain

A schedule is more than just a timeline.

It is a communication instrument that defines when accountability must occur.

Use the schedule domain to:

- sequence dependencies,

- clarify commitments,

- signal delays early,

- align stakeholder expectations,

- and define review points for risk, ethics, and performance validation.

In AI and digital projects, the impact of decisions often extends beyond development to include deployment, consequences, and sustained usage.

Responsible scheduling, therefore, includes:

- post-deployment monitoring milestones,

- performance validation checkpoints,

- and structured review cycles for unintended impacts.

A visible schedule builds trust.

An unmanaged schedule leads to unexpected issues, especially when consequences emerge after delivery.

3.1.4 Financial Performance Domain

Projects must plan resource commitments deliberately, authorize expenditures transparently, and continuously demonstrate that spending delivers measurable value.

Use this domain to ensure that:

- budgets reflect realistic scope and risk assumptions,

- costs are tracked with visible accountability,

- forecasts are updated as conditions change,

- financial decisions remain aligned with strategic objectives.

In AI and digital environments, cost structures extend beyond traditional labor and capital expenditures.

Leaders must be accountable for:

- cloud consumption and ongoing operational expenses,

- model training and computational energy costs,

- data acquisition, licensing, and representativeness costs

- stakeholder engagement and oversight mechanisms.

High-performance systems may carry substantial environmental and infrastructure costs. Financial discipline, therefore, includes evaluating whether technical ambition is proportionate to business value and societal impact.

In cloud-enabled and platform-based environments, expenses continue beyond the go-live phase. Financial oversight must extend to sustained usage monitoring, energy consumption awareness, and long-term value realization.

3.1.5   Risk Performance Domain

Risk management is a structured approach to foresight.

Use this domain to:

- identify exposure early,

- assess likelihood and impact,

- distinguish internal from external uncertainty,

- define mitigation and contingency,

- monitor emerging threats throughout the lifecycle.

Projects face both internal risks—such as design errors, bias, and performance failures—and external risks, including market volatility, regulatory shifts, and competitive pressures. Effective risk management requires evaluating exposure in relation to both value objectives and ethical considerations.

In AI projects, risks extend beyond cost and schedule variances. They may also include:

- biased or inaccurate model outputs,

- misuse or unintended application,

- regulatory non-compliance,

- reputational and societal harm.

AI risk management is not static. It may require retraining models, refining datasets, implementing control mechanisms, or reassessing system behavior after deployment.

Ignoring risk does not eliminate it. Under delivery pressure, unmanaged risks compound, and accountability weakens.

Structured risk governance enhances resilience and protects long-term value.

3.1.6   Stakeholder Performance Domain

Stakeholders influence an organization's legitimacy.

Use this domain to ensure the following:

- influence and impact are systematically mapped,

- expectations are clarified and documented,

- engagement strategies reflect both power and vulnerability,

- harm potential is evaluated and escalated when necessary.

Stakeholder discipline protects reputation, reduces resistance, and strengthens long-term trust.

This domain addresses stakeholder management as an operational responsibility throughout the project lifecycle. A comprehensive framework for stakeholder analysis, prioritization, and protection is presented in Chapter 8.

3.1.7   Resource Performance Domain

Resources are not limited to people alone.

They include:

- team capability,

- vendor alignment,

- infrastructure availability,

- digital tools.

In AI and digital projects, resource strength depends not only on capacity but also on capability and composition.

Effective resource management requires:

- multidisciplinary expertise,

- sufficient technical competence,

- diversity of perspective to reduce bias,

- representation of affected stakeholders where appropriate,

- and clear assignment of responsibility and accountability.

Specialized systems, particularly AI models, create transparency gaps between sponsors and technical teams. Without clear role definitions and structured accountability frameworks (e.g., RACI), the risks of moral hazard and misuse increase.

Alignment among responsibility, authority, and competence determines execution strength.

Strong resources not only deliver faster; they also deliver more reliably.

3.1.8 Quality Performance Domain

Quality is built in, not inspected at the end.

However, quality is also negotiated under pressure.

When timelines tighten or cost constraints become more stringent, leaders must manage trade-offs between quality and other performance domains.

Use this domain to:

- define acceptance criteria early,

- clarify non-negotiable standards,

- make trade-offs explicit and approved,

- monitor quality impacts throughout delivery.

Common trade-offs include:

- accuracy vs. development cost,

- explainability vs. intellectual property protection,

- flexibility vs. legal safeguards,

- speed vs. regulatory compliance,

- business benefit vs. societal impact.

Under delivery pressure, quality erosion is rarely acknowledged; it tends to be incremental and selective.

When trade-offs are documented and governed, performance remains defensible.

When trade-offs are implicit, accountability weakens, and long-term exposure increases.

Quality failures often stem from earlier governance failures rather than solely from technical deficiencies.

3.2 Expanded Domains for Modern Projects

Digital transformation and AI-driven systems introduce explicit structural responsibilities that traditional models often address implicitly.

In complex digital and AI environments, two additional domains must be explicitly defined.

They are not extensions.

They are requirements.

3.2.1 Ethics Management Performance Domain

Projects increasingly incorporate value judgments.

This domain ensures that leaders:

- align value creation with ethical principles,

- prevent foreseeable harm,

- protect fundamental rights,

- establish misconduct escalation mechanisms,

- document ethical decision logic.

Ethics must be managed proactively, not reactively.

When efficiency takes precedence over ethics, legitimacy collapses.

3.2.2 Digital Asset and Record Governance Performance Domain

Modern projects generate continuous streams of digital artifacts:

- logs,

- models,

- contracts,

- configurations,

- analytical outputs.

Without disciplined control, these artifacts become sources of unmanaged risk exposure.

Leaders must clearly define:

- ownership,

- retention policies,

- access controls,

- traceability mechanisms,

- audit readiness standards.

If digital governance begins late, accountability fails early.

Traceability is essential in regulated and AI-driven environments.

3.3 Using the Domains as a System

Performance domains do not operate independently.

In practice:

- Weak governance undermines scope discipline.

- Poor digital asset control increases ethical exposure.

- Inadequate stakeholder management escalates risk.

- Financial opacity erodes trust.

Leaders must view the domains as an interconnected system of controls.

The question is not:

> Have we addressed each domain?

The question is:

> Are these domains reinforcing one another?

3.4   A Leadership Perspective

Managing performance domains is not merely administrative overhead.

It is structured leadership.

At any point in the lifecycle, leaders should ask themselves:

- Are the decision rights clearly defined?

- Are the risks visible and assigned to an owner?

- Are stakeholders protected?

- Are digital artifacts traceable?

- Are the ethical implications documented?

Modern project management is not only about delivering outputs but also about delivering value responsibly, defensibly, and sustainably across all performance domains.

The domains provide structure. Leadership empowers them to be effective.

Part II

Delivering in Digital and Intelligent Environments

Chapter 4

Project Life Cycles: Predictive, Agile, and Hybrid

Projects follow different life cycle approaches depending on factors such as uncertainty, complexity, regulatory requirements, and stakeholder expectations.

There are three predominant life cycle models used in complex digital and AI project environments:

- Predictive

- Agile

- Hybrid

Understanding when and how to use each approach is a key leadership responsibility within the project management performance domains.

4.1 Predictive Life Cycle

The predictive life cycle is often called "traditional" project management.

It assumes that:

- Requirements can be defined early

- Scope can be clearly documented

- Work can be sequenced logically

- Change should be controlled

Predictive projects typically follow several stages, such as:

- Initiation

- Planning

- Execution

- Monitoring and Controlling

- Closing

This approach works well when:

- Requirements are stable

- Regulatory documentation is required

- Physical assets are being built

- Contracts are fixed

However, predictive methods struggle when requirements evolve quickly or when innovation is required.

4.2 Agile Life Cycle

Agile emerged as a response to rigid, documentation-heavy methodologies that were not well-suited to adapting to change.

Instead of defining everything upfront, agile assumes:

- Change is normal

- Customers learn as the project progresses

- Solutions evolve through iteration

- Collaboration creates better outcomes

Agile work is delivered in short cycles, often called iterations or sprints.

Each cycle includes:

- Planning

- Development

- Review

- Reflection

This allows teams to adjust quickly based on feedback.

4.3   The Agile Manifesto: Core Principles

Agile is guided by the Agile Manifesto, which emphasizes four core values:

- Individuals and interactions over processes and tools

- Working solutions over comprehensive documentation

- Customer collaboration over contract negotiation

- Responding to change rather than strictly following a fixed plan

These values do not exclude planning or documentation.

Instead, they prioritize flexibility, effective communication, and delivering value.

In practical terms, this means:

- Teams communicate frequently

- Stakeholders provide regular feedback

- Progress is demonstrated often

- Plans are adjusted as needed

Agility is not the absence of discipline; it is disciplined adaptability.

4.4 Scrum: The Most Widely Used Agile Framework

Scrum is the most commonly used agile framework.

It provides a simple structure for iterative delivery.

Scrum includes three primary roles:

- Product Owner

- Scrum Master

- Development Team

Product Owner Defines priorities and represents the interests of stakeholders.

Scrum Master Facilitates the process and removes obstacles.

Development Team Delivers functional increments during each sprint.

Scrum also defines structured events:

- Sprint Planning

- Daily Stand-ups

- Sprint Review

- Sprint Retrospective

These ceremonies create transparency and continuous improvement.

Scrum is simple by design; however, simplicity does not eliminate the need for governance.

4.5 The Role of the Project Manager in Agile Environments

Traditional agile literature does not always include a formal "project manager" role.

However, in complex, regulated, or large-scale environments, project management responsibilities remain essential.

They evolve.

Even in agile contexts, someone must ensure:

- Budget oversight

- Risk coordination

- Vendor management

- Regulatory compliance

- Cross-team alignment

- Executive reporting

These responsibilities fall within the project management performance domains.

In some organizations:

- The Scrum Master performs various coordination tasks.

- The Product Owner manages stakeholder alignment.

- A program or delivery manager oversees financial governance.

A project manager works alongside agile team members.

The key principle is as follows:

Agile eliminates rigid command-and-control structures but does not remove accountability.

4.6 Hybrid Life Cycles: Tailoring for Reality

Most real-world projects are neither purely predictive nor purely agile in nature.

They are hybrids.

Hybrid means deliberately combining elements of both approaches.

For example:

- Predictive governance with agile delivery

- Fixed budgets with iterative scope management

- Stage-gate approvals integrated with sprint cycles

- Regulatory documentation with incremental releases

Hybrid is not confusing.

It is tailoring.

Projects operate within constraints:

- Regulatory obligations

- Financial approvals

- Contractual commitments

- Organizational culture

Pure agile may conflict with these constraints.

Purely predictive approaches may reduce adaptability.

Hybrid systems allow for balance.

4.7 Why Tailoring Matters

Research and practice show that no single method is suitable for every project.

Successful organizations tailor their life cycle approach based on:

- Project complexity

- Risk level

- Stakeholder expectations

- Industry regulation

- Organizational maturity

- Speed-to-market pressure

Tailoring requires conscious design and is a decision within the domain of governance performance.

Without tailoring:

- Agile becomes uncontrolled change.

- Predictive becomes rigid bureaucracy.

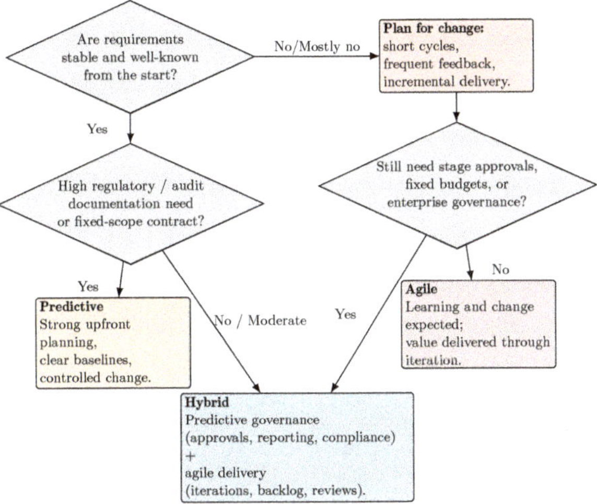

Tip: If answers are mixed, choose Hybrid and document what is agile, what is predictive, and why.

Figure 4.1: Decision tree for selecting a predictive, agile, or hybrid project life cycle

With tailoring:

- Structure supports adaptability.

- Governance protects innovation.

4.8   Choosing the Right Approach

Project leaders should ask the following questions:

- How stable are our requirements?

- How quickly must we deliver value?

- What regulatory constraints apply?

- How mature is our organization in agile practices?

- What level of uncertainty exists?

The answers guide the design of the life cycle.

Modern project management is not about choosing sides; it is about designing the right balance.

4.9   Key Takeaways

- **Life cycle choice is a governance design decision.** Selecting predictive, agile, or hybrid approaches is not merely a technical preference but a strategic decision that shapes authority, accountability, control mechanisms, and performance outcomes throughout the project lifecycle.

- **Predictive and agile approaches optimize for different risk profiles.** Predictive methods provide stability, thorough documentation, and regulatory defensibility. Conversely, agile methods provide adaptability, learning velocity, and early value realization. Each approach addresses different dimensions of uncertainty.

- **Agility does not eliminate the need for governance.** Even in iterative environments, budget oversight, risk coordination, compliance obligations, and stakeholder accountability remain essential. Flexibility without governance leads to unmanaged exposure.

- **Hybrid is a deliberate architecture, not a compromise.** Combining predictive governance with agile delivery allows organizations to balance innovation with institutional control. Effective hybrid models are consciously designed, not improvised.

- **Tailoring is a leadership responsibility.** Project leaders must evaluate uncertainty, regulatory demands, organizational maturity, and stakeholder expectations before defining the life cycle structure. Failure to tailor the approach can result in either rigid bureaucracy or uncontrolled change.

- **Life cycle structure influences performance across all domains.** The chosen approach affects stakeholder engagement, risk exposure, information governance, financial oversight, and long-term sustainability. Therefore, life cycle design directly shapes enterprise-level outcomes.

Life cycle architecture determines how governance, responsibility, integrity, and performance are structured throughout execution. It establishes the control logic that later domains—digital, AI, stakeholder, and governance systems—must reinforce.

Project leaders should confirm the following.

Leadership Checklist: Life Cycle Selection

☐ The selected life cycle reflects project uncertainty, regulatory exposure, and delivery risk.

☐ Governance authority, escalation paths, and documentation expectations are clearly defined.

☐ Trade-offs between predictive and agile approaches have been evaluated and a rationale recorded.

☐ Governance mechanisms remain in place even when iterative delivery methods are used.

☐ Hybrid approaches are intentionally designed rather than improvised.

☐ The life cycle structure supports stakeholder oversight, risk management, and long-term sustainability.

☐ Tailoring decision documented; decision criteria (requirements stability, regulatory need) confirmed.

Chapter 5

Managing Projects in a Cloud and Digital Environment

Cloud and digital technologies are not solely technical topics. They are project delivery environments.

Today, most projects operate within a digital ecosystem:

- Teams collaborate online

- Systems are hosted externally

- Documents are stored on shared platforms

- Deliverables are deployed continuously

- Data flows across organizational boundaries

The project managers responsibility is not to engineer these systems. It is intended to manage how they are governed, controlled, and aligned with value.

5.1 From Infrastructure Projects to Platform Projects

In traditional projects, infrastructure was stable and internal. Today, infrastructure is often external and flexible.

This shift brings significant changes:

- Cost structures (from capital expense to operating expense)

- Risk ownership

- Security responsibilities

- Contract management

- Oversight mechanisms

The project manager must incorporate cloud platforms and digital tools into the projects governance model.

5.2 Why This Matters for Project Success

Cloud and digital environments offer numerous advantages:

- Faster setup

- Easier scaling

- Remote collaboration

- Shorter release cycles

However, they also introduce project risks:

- Uncontrolled spending

- Ambiguous accountability

- Data protection violations

- Vendor dependency

- Reduced visibility for sponsors

Projects fail not because of the technology itself, but because governance and control mechanisms are unclear or inadequate.

5.3 Project Management Responsibilities in a Digital Environment

Cloud and digital technologies affect nearly every domain of project management performance.

5.3.1 Governance Domain

The sponsor must understand the following:

- Who owns the data?

- Who approves configuration changes?

- What risks are transferred to suppliers?

- What internal risks remain?

The project manager ensures that these decisions are documented and approved promptly.

5.3.2 Scope Domain

Digital platforms can easily expand their scope.

New features can be added quickly and efficiently. This flexibility can lead to uncontrolled growth.

Project managers must:

- Define clear scope boundaries

- Use structured backlog management

- Monitor feature expansion against business value

5.3.3 Cost Domain

Cloud services often charge based on usage.

This means:

- Costs increase as usage increases

- Poor configuration increases expenses

- Delays extend operational charges

Project managers must integrate usage monitoring into financial control processes.

5.3.4 Risk Domain

Digital risks include:

- Service interruption

- Data breaches

- Regulatory non-compliance

- Loss of intellectual property

These elements must be explicitly included in the risk register.

5.4 Digital Collaboration and Accountability

Modern project teams rarely work from a single location.

Digital collaboration platforms enhance:

- Transparency

- Traceability

- Documentation

But they also create:

- Information overload

- Miscommunication

- Tool fragmentation

The project manager should:

- Define one primary communication channel

- Define document storage standards

- Clarify the rules for version control

- Establish clear expectations for documentation discipline

Digital tools do not replace leadership; they amplify it.

5.5 Vendor and Supplier Management in Cloud Projects

Cloud projects often involve external providers.

This shifts the project focus from internal coordination to inter-organizational management.

The project manager must ensure the following:

- Clear service agreements

- Defined escalation paths

- Performance monitoring

- Exit strategies

Vendor lock-in is a strategic risk that should be addressed at the sponsor level.

5.6 Integration with the Digital Asset and Record Governance Domain

Digital platforms generate large volumes of:

- Logs

- Decision records

- Configuration histories

- Data artifacts

Without structured governance:

- Decisions cannot be reconstructed

- Compliance audits fail

- AI reuse becomes impossible

The project manager must ensure that:

- Record retention is defined at the initiation stage

- Access controls are documented

- Change histories are preserved

- Archive procedures are planned at the time of closure

5.7   Real-World Example

A financial services organization migrated its regulatory reporting system to a cloud environment.

The project was delivered quickly and within budget.

However:

- Usage costs doubled after go-live

- Access rights were poorly defined

- Data transfer between sites was prone to cybersecurity attacks

- Audit documentation was incomplete

The technology worked as intended.

Governance has failed.

After restructuring the oversight mechanisms and implementing cost monitoring controls, the project stabilized.

Lesson: Digital success requires management discipline rather than technical expertise.

5.8 Practical Checklist for Project Managers

Before approving cloud or digital tools, ensure the following:

Table 5.1: Digital Environment Checklist

Confirm that the following controls are established within the digital delivery environment:

- ☐ Data ownership formally defined.
- ☐ Costs monitored and forecasted.
- ☐ Access rights documented and formally approved.
- ☐ Clear escalation path defined for system outages.
- ☐ Compliance requirements identified and reviewed.
- ☐ Vendor dependencies formally assessed.

5.9 Leadership in a Digital Project Context

In a digital environment, project managers must:

- Ask governance questions early

- Prevent uncontrolled tool expansion

- Maintain sponsor visibility

- Protect organizational data

- Align digital flexibility with strategic objectives

Cloud and digital technologies enhance speed and efficiency.

However, speed without governance increases risk.

Modern project management involves balancing flexibility with structure.

5.10 Key Takeaways

- **Digital environments are governance environments.** Cloud platforms, collaboration tools, and shared data ecosystems are redefining cost structures, risk allocation, and accountability boundaries. Technology choices have become integral to governance design decisions.

- **External infrastructure shifts responsibility, but not accountability.** While operational control may reside with cloud providers or digital vendors, ultimate responsibility for compliance, cost discipline, and data protection remains with the sponsoring organization.

- **Cost visibility must evolve alongside operating expense models.** Usage-based pricing requires continuous financial monitoring. Without structured oversight, digital flexibility can silently convert into uncontrolled operational risk.

- **Digital speed amplifies both value and risk.** Faster deployment cycles and collaboration tools enhance responsiveness; however, they also amplify scope creep, vendor dependency, and regulatory risks when governance mechanisms are unclear.

- **Digital asset and record governance constitute a performance domain.** Logs, decision histories, configuration records, and access controls form the evidentiary backbone of defensible project delivery. Without structured retention and traceability, auditability and AI reuse become impossible.

- **Leadership discipline determines digital success.** Cloud and digital tools enable performance; however, only structured oversight, clearly defined ownership, and documented control mechanisms ensure sustainable outcomes.

Digital project environments intensify the governance architecture defined by the project life cycle. Managing cloud-enabled projects is not merely an IT capability; it represents the structural reinforcement of governance, accountability, integrity, and performance within distributed ecosystems.

Project leaders should confirm the following.

Leadership Checklist: Digital Environment Governance

- ☐ Cloud and platform architecture decisions are evaluated as governance decisions.
- ☐ Organizational accountability for compliance, cost management, and data protection remains clearly assigned.
- ☐ Usage-based pricing models are supported by continuous financial monitoring.
- ☐ Vendor dependencies, access controls, and platform risks are documented and monitored.
- ☐ Digital asset and record governance exists for logs, configuration changes, and decision histories.
- ☐ Digital speed and collaboration operate within clearly defined governance boundaries.
- ☐ Vendor exit strategies have been assessed and discussed at sponsor level.

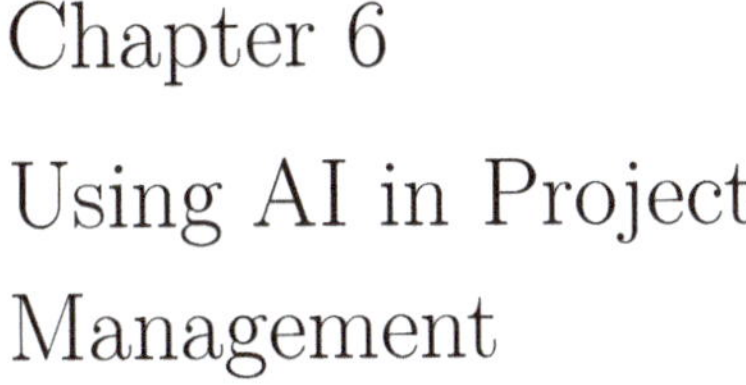

Chapter 6

Using AI in Project Management

Artificial Intelligence (AI) is transforming the way projects are planned, monitored, and delivered.

However, AI is not magic. It is not human intelligence in digital form.

It is a set of computational techniques that:

- Learn patterns from data

- Generate predictions

- Produce structured outputs

- Support decision-making

When used correctly, AI strengthens multiple domains of project management performance.

This chapter explains the following:

- What AI is

- How it differs from earlier systems

- How AI can improve project performance

- How to apply it responsibly

6.1 What AI Really Is

In practical terms, AI systems replicate specific human capabilities, such as:

- Language generation

- Pattern recognition

- Classification

- Forecasting

- Recommendation

Unlike traditional software, AI systems learn from data.

Earlier decision-support systems relied on fixed rules. If the situation changed, the system needed to be manually reprogrammed.

Modern AI systems:

- Adapt based on data patterns

- Generate probabilistic outputs

- Improve through training

However, they do not:

- Understand truth as humans do

- Possess moral reasoning

- Hold accountability

They assist but do not replace leadership.

6.2 Automation–Autonomy Continuum

AI systems exist along a continuum.

Some only automate repetitive tasks. Others can execute sequences of actions with minimal supervision.

Selecting the level of autonomy is a governance decision.

Higher autonomy requires stronger control measures.

6.3 How AI Strengthens Project Performance

AI can enhance several domains of project management performance.

6.3.1 Planning and Forecasting

AI can:

- Analyze historical project data

- Predict delays

- Identify cost variance patterns

- Detect schedule conflicts

This improves early intervention efforts.

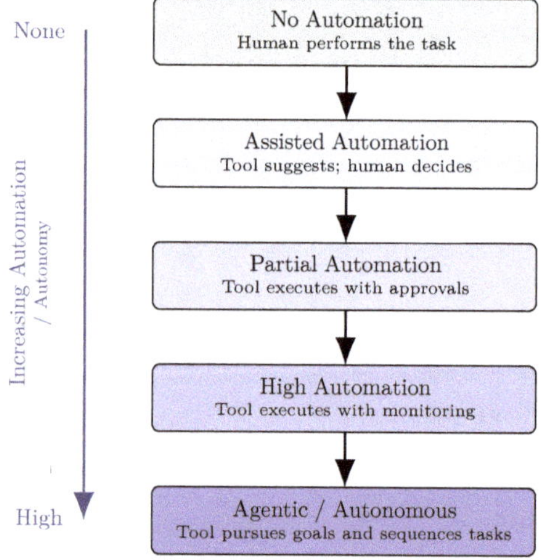

Project guidance: Treat the selected autonomy level as a governance decision. Higher autonomy increases the need for documented controls, monitoring, escalation paths, and clear responsibility.

Figure 6.1: Automation–Autonomy continuum for AI systems

6.3.2   Risk Identification

AI tools can detect:

- Emerging financial irregularities

- Supplier instability signals

- Contract anomalies

- Scope creep trends

AI expands pattern recognition but does not replace the responsibility of risk ownership.

6.3.3   Communication and Reporting

Generative AI can:

- Draft executive summaries

- Summarize meetings

- Generate dashboards

- Translate complex reports

This increases efficiency but requires a review.

6.3.4   Knowledge and Documentation

AI can:

- Extract lessons learned

- Organize decision logs

- Improve the searchability of records

- Support structured archiving

This strengthens the performance domain of Digital Asset and Record Governance.

6.4   Leadership Principles for Using AI in Projects

When integrating AI tools into project management:

- Define clear use cases

- Hold humans accountable

- Validate outputs before taking action

- Monitor overreliance

- Document decision rationales

AI enhances performance but does not transfer responsibility.

6.5 Key Takeaways

- **AI integration in project management increases decision velocity and exposure simultaneously.** Automation of forecasting, reporting, and risk analysis enhances performance but also increases reliance on algorithmic outputs, requiring structured oversight.

- **Human judgment remains the accountability anchor.** AI may support prioritization and prediction, but ultimate authority and ethical responsibility remain with clearly identifiable human roles.

- **Algorithmic tools require governance design rather than mere adoption enthusiasm.** Before deploying AI in project environments, organizations must establish approval thresholds, override mechanisms, and documentation standards.

- **AI amplifies existing governance strengths and weaknesses.** In mature governance systems, AI enhances transparency and foresight. However, in weak systems, it accelerates error propagation and obscures accountability.

- **Organizational maturity determines safe AI adoption.** Effective use of AI in project management requires established escalation paths, traceability controls, digital asset governance, and clearly defined accountability.

Using AI in project management represents an evolution in governance maturity. Organizations that integrate AI within a disciplined governance architecture strengthen performance, while those that adopt AI without structural safeguards amplify systemic risk. In this context, AI adoption serves as a test of an organizations alignment with the GRIP Framework.

Project leaders should confirm the following.

Leadership Checklist: AI Usage

☐ AI-supported forecasting, prioritization, or reporting tools have defined oversight procedures.

☐ Human decision authority remains clearly assigned.

☐ Approval thresholds and override mechanisms exist for AI-supported decisions.

☐ Algorithmic outputs influencing decisions remain traceable and reviewable.

☐ Escalation paths, traceability controls, and accountability assignments are confirmed before AI tools are adopted.

☐ The selected level of AI autonomy has been treated as a governance decision, with controls proportional to that level.

☐ Reliance on AI outputs is monitored and decision rationales are documented.

Chapter 7

Managing AI Projects

Building or deploying an AI system is fundamentally different from implementing traditional software.

AI systems:

- Depend heavily on data

- May produce probabilistic outputs

- Can be difficult to explain

- May affect individuals and society

These characteristics expand governance exposure, ethical risks, and accountability obligations.

In many regions, AI is no longer governed solely by internal policies. Regulatory and standards frameworks are emerging to formalize expectations for risk management, transparency, and oversight. The European Union (EU) AI Act establishes binding, risk-based obligations for high-risk systems, including requirements for documentation, logging, human oversight, and lifecycle monitoring (European

Union, 2024). The NIST AI Risk Management Framework emphasizes structured governance, explainability, defined risk tolerance, and documented oversight processes (Tabassi, 2023). Additionally, ISO/IEC 42001:2023 Information Technology - Artificial Intelligence - Management System introduces a certifiable management system standard requiring organizations to establish, implement, maintain, and continually improve structured AI governance processes (International Standards Organization, 2023).

These frameworks do not introduce any new principles. They formalize what responsible leadership already demands: AI systems must be designed as accountable architectures from inception through sustained operation. Managing AI projects today, therefore, requires structured governance, traceability, and defensible decision-making capable of adapting to evolving regulatory environments and management system requirements.

7.1 Why AI Projects Are Different

7.1.1 Opacity and Explainability

AI models can function as complex statistical systems.

Outputs may not be easily explainable.

This affects:

- Regulatory defensibility

- Stakeholder trust

- Audit transparency

7.1.2 Delayed Impact

AI decisions can continue to influence users long after deployment.

Consequences may:

- Affect vulnerable populations

- Reinforce bias

- Shape financial or legal outcomes

This creates a gap between design decisions and their consequences.

7.1.3 Diffusion of Responsibility

AI projects involve:

- Data engineers

- Model developers

- Vendors

- Business owners

- End-users

- Cloud providers

Without structured mapping, responsibility becomes diffused, and ownership remains unclear.

7.2 Implications for Project Management Performance Domains

AI systems change how performance domains must be exercised.

Governance can no longer focus only on delivery approval. It must define autonomy levels, override authority, acceptance criteria, and escalation thresholds. Research on AI project accountability confirms that when delivery pressure increases, ethical and compliance oversight often become the first controls to weaken unless governance is deliberately reinforced.[1]

Risk management must extend beyond merely cost and schedule variances. It must address bias exposure, misuse scenarios, systemic harm, and reputational risks.

Digital asset and record governance become foundational. Model versioning, data lineage, configuration control, and decision logs constitute the evidentiary foundation of accountability.

Ethics management is transitioning from an advisory review role to operational control. AI systems inherently incorporate value judgments. Ethical guardrails, oversight triggers, and misconduct pathways must, therefore, be integrated into the system architecture.

Clear accountability mapping across problem definition, data sourcing, model design, monitoring, and incident response is essential. Appendix C provides a structured AI Project Responsibility Framework and an audit checklist.

Responsibility assignments must be reviewed at initiation, design approval, deployment, and post-deployment phases to prevent accountability drift.

7.3 Human Accountability in AI-Influenced Decisions

When AI influences or automates decisions, human accountability remains intact.

Override authority must remain identifiable, over-reliance should be monitored, and escalation pathways must be clearly defined.

AI may recommend or execute actions, but the responsibility remains with humans.

7.4 Key Takeaways

- **AI projects are governance-intensive systems.** Opacity, probabilistic outputs, and societal impact extend oversight requirements beyond those of traditional software delivery. AI initiatives must be structured as accountability architectures rather than merely technical implementations.

- **Autonomy increases governance obligations.** As systems transition from decision support to autonomous execution, clarity of authority, escalation mechanisms, and override designs must increase proportionally. Reduced human intervention does not reduce human responsibility.

- **Explainability and traceability are essential performance requirements.** Model versioning, data lineage, decision logs, and monitoring thresholds are more than just technical artifacts; they serve as the evidentiary foundation for regulatory defensibility and stakeholder trust.

- **Delayed and distributed impacts require lifecycle accountability.** AI consequences may emerge long after deployment and across organizational boundaries. Therfore, responsibility must extend to monitoring, drift detection, and post-implementation review.

- **Ethical controls must be embedded in system design.** AI systems embed value judgments through data selection, objective functions, and deployment contexts. Ensuring ethical alignment requires documented guardrails, bias testing, and structured review mechanisms.

- **Responsibilities must be explicitly mapped and regularly reviewed.** Without clearly assigned accountability for problem definition, data sourcing, model design, oversight, and incident response, the diffusion of responsibility becomes inevitable.

- **Human accountability is non-transferable.** AI may recommend or automate actions, but moral, legal, and organizational responsibility remains with identifiable human roles and governing institutions.

AI initiatives require the full implementation of governance, responsibility, integrity, and performance controls throughout the entire lifecycle. In this context, AI projects represent the most governance-intensive application of the GRIP Framework.

Project leaders should confirm the following.

Leadership Checklist: AI Project Governance

- ☐ Governance structures reflect the higher oversight requirements of AI systems.
- ☐ Escalation mechanisms and override authority increase with system autonomy.
- ☐ Model versioning, data lineage, and decision logs are maintained.
- ☐ Monitoring processes exist for model drift and unintended outcomes.
- ☐ Ethical guardrails, bias testing, and fairness reviews are embedded in system design.
- ☐ Responsibilities across problem definition, data sourcing, development, and monitoring are clearly assigned.
- ☐ Human accountability for system outcomes remains explicitly documented.
- ☐ The AI responsibility structure is formally reviewed and reapproved at initiation, design approval, go-live, and post-deployment review.

Part III

Governance, Stakeholders, and Integration

Chapter 8

Stakeholder Excellence

Projects operate within networks of people, institutions, and affected communities.

A project is not only a technical or financial endeavor. It is a social system embedded within power structures, expectations, and accountability relationships.

Stakeholder excellence is fundamental to achieving high performance across all project management domains.

8.1   What Is a Stakeholder?

A stakeholder is any individual, group, or organization that:

- Influences the project, or

- Is affected—directly or indirectly—by its outcomes.

Stakeholders may include:

- Sponsors and executives

- Customers and users

- Team members

- Suppliers and vendors

- Regulators

- Investors

- Communities

- Employees indirectly affected

In digital and AI projects, additional stakeholders often emerge:

- Individuals whose personal data are collected or processed ("data subjects")

- Impacted communities

- Advocacy groups

- Future or downstream users

Stakeholders are defined by their impact and influence, not by contractual relationships.

8.2   Why Stakeholder Management Matters

Projects fail more often due to misaligned expectations and unmanaged resistance than because of technical deficiencies.

Weak stakeholder engagement leads to:

- Resistance and obstruction

- Scope conflict

- Delayed decisions or approvals

- Reputational damage

- Erosion of trust

Strong stakeholder discipline builds:

- Strategic alignment

- Transparency

- Shared accountability

- Legitimacy and trust

Trust is not a soft variable; it is a governance asset.

8.3 Modern Stakeholder Analysis Dimensions

Traditional power-interest grids remain useful but are insufficient for digitally accountable environments.

Modern stakeholder analysis should consider the following factors (Miller, 2022; Mitchell et al., 1997):

Power

Ability to influence funding, direction, continuation, or termination.

Legitimacy

Validity and moral standing of the stakeholders claim.

Urgency

Time sensitivity and the criticality of concerns.

Harm Potential

Risk of negative impacts if the project fails, malfunctions, or produces unintended consequences.

Harm potential is especially significant in digital and AI systems. Low-power stakeholders may face significant risks, even when they lack formal influence.

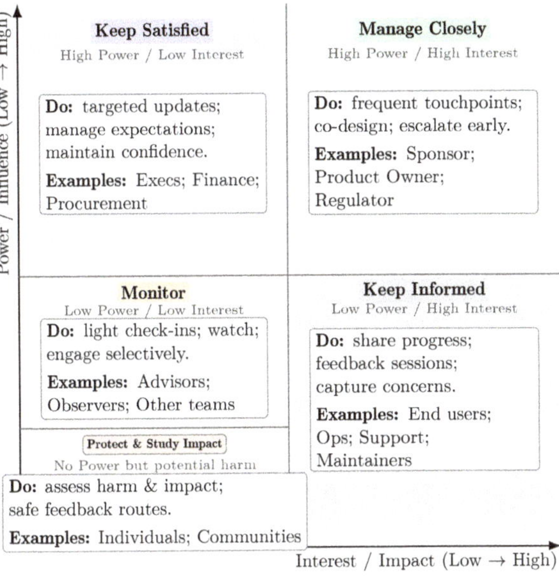

Note: low power does not imply low exposure–prioritize protection when harm potential is high.

Figure 8.1: Stakeholder mapping quadrant for engagement planning, extended with a low-power / high-harm category.

8.4 Structured Stakeholder Analysis Process

Stakeholder analysis is not a one-time exercise; it must evolve alongside the project.

Step 1: Identify

Systematically identify all influencing and affected parties, including indirect and downstream stakeholders.

Step 2: Assess

Evaluate stakeholders based on their power, legitimacy, urgency, and potential for harm.

Step 3: Prioritize

Determine the level of engagement intensity and the necessary protection requirements.

High-risk stakeholder exposure should prompt governance-level visibility and escalation.

Step 4: Plan Engagement

Define communication cadence, escalation pathways, and protection mechanisms as required.

8.5   Stakeholder Mapping

Figure 8.1 extends the traditional power-interest grid by incorporating a distinct category for low-power stakeholders who have high potential to cause harm.

8.6 Key Takeaways

- **Stakeholder boundaries extend beyond contractual relationships.** Stakeholders extend beyond formal authority structures; they are defined by their impact and influence, not by organizational charts.

- **Harm potential elevates moral and governance priority.** Low-power stakeholders who face high exposure to risk require structured protection mechanisms. Influence alone is an insufficient criterion for prioritization in digitally accountable environments.

- **Stakeholder analysis is a governance instrument, not merely a communication tool.** A structured evaluation of power, legitimacy, urgency, and potential harm determines oversight intensity, escalation design, and accountability mapping.

- **Trust functions as institutional capital.** Transparent engagement, documented responsiveness, and visible fairness strengthen long-term legitimacy. A loss of trust increases regulatory exposure, reputational risk, and operational challenges.

- **Engagement strategies must address both influence and vulnerability.** Projects that focus only on powerful actors risk overlooking downstream impacts that may later generate resistance, compliance failures, or societal backlash.

- **Stakeholder excellence requires deliberate lifecycle integration.** Identification, prioritization, and protection mechanisms must be revisited during initiation, design, deployment, and post-implementation review phases rather than treated as a one-time planning activity.

Stakeholder excellence operationalizes the Responsibility and Integrity dimensions of the GRIP Framework by aligning influence, vulnerability, and accountability throughout the lifecycle, particularly in situations where power and the potential for harm diverge.

Project leaders should confirm the following.

Leadership Checklist: Stakeholder Accountability

- ☐ Stakeholders are identified based on impact and influence.
- ☐ Stakeholders are assessed across power, legitimacy, urgency, and harm potential not power and interest alone.
- ☐ Low-power stakeholders with high potential harm receive structured protection.
- ☐ Stakeholder analysis informs governance intensity and escalation design.
- ☐ Engagement strategies address both influence and vulnerability.
- ☐ Stakeholder engagement decisions, escalation actions, and protection measures are documented.
- ☐ Stakeholder evaluation is revisited during initiation, design, deployment, and post-implementation review.

Chapter 9

Governance Excellence

Governance defines how authority, accountability, and control operate within a project.

While stakeholder management focuses on relationships, governance focuses on structure.

Both are necessary; they are not interchangeable.

9.1　What Is Governance?

Governance establishes:

- Who makes decisions

- What information is required

- How approvals are granted

- How risks are escalated

- How performance is monitored

- How accountability is enforced

Governance operates within the domain of governance performance.

It ensures that the project:

- Aligns with strategy

- Protects resources

- Meets regulatory obligations

- Delivers the intended value

Governance is structured accountability.

9.2 Governance Structures in Practice

Common governance mechanisms include:

- Steering committees

- Stage-gate approvals

- Risk review boards

- Sponsor checkpoints

- Audit reviews

Each structure should define:

- Decision authority

- Escalation path

- Documentation requirement

- Reporting cadence

9.3   Role Clarity Through RACI

Ambiguity undermines effective governance.

RACI clarifies:

- Responsible Executes the task

- Accountable Owns the result

- Consulted Provides input

- Informed Receives updates

Only one person should be accountable for each major decision.

Appendix C provides a structured AI Project Responsibility Framework and an audit checklist to support the assignment of accountability in managing AI projects.

RACI Template

Table 9.1: R-A-C-I Template

Task	R	A	C	I
Model Approval	Data Lead	Sponsor	Legal	Team
Go-Live Decision	Project Manager	Sponsor	Risk, Security	Stake-hold-ers

9.4   Governance as a System

Governance interacts with all domains of project management performance:

- It defines the scope of approval.

- It approves budget allocations.

- It escalates risk.

- It enforces ethical guardrails.

- It validates digital asset and record governance controls.

Without governance, domains operate independently.

With governance, they operate as a cohesive system.

9.5 Balancing Governance and Agility

Excessive lack of governance creates chaos.

Excessive governance creates paralysis.

Effective governance:

- Scales with project complexity

- Matches regulatory exposure

- Protects innovation without suffocating it

Governance excellence enables agility; it does not block it.

9.6 Key Takeaways

- **Governance is structured accountability.** It defines who holds decision-making authority, what evidence is required, how risks are escalated, and how performance is monitored. Without an explicit structure, accountability becomes diffused and unenforceable.

- **Governance integrates all performance domains.** Scope approval, budget allocation, risk escalation, ethical oversight, and digital asset governance are not isolated controls; governance integrates them into a coherent decision-making system.

- **Role clarity prevents responsibility diffusion.** A clear RACI assignment, particularly designating a single accountable owner for each major decision, protects projects from ambiguity, delays, and reputational risks.

- **Governance must scale with increasing complexity and exposure.** Projects with higher regulatory risk, greater digital dependency, or significant societal impact require proportionally stronger oversight mechanisms and well-documented control structures.

- **Effective governance enables agility.** Disciplined authority structures allow teams to adapt quickly within clearly defined boundaries. Agility without governance leads to unmanaged risk, while governance without proportionality results in inertia.

- **Trust emerges from visible accountability.** When decision rights, escalation paths, and documentation requirements are transparent, stakeholder confidence increases, and long-term legitimacy is strengthened.

Governance excellence operationalizes the Governance and Responsibility pillars of the GRIP Framework by transforming authority, escalation, and oversight into a comprehensive, lifecycle-spanning control architecture that integrates all performance domains into a cohesive system.

Project leaders should confirm the following.

Leadership Checklist: Governance Structure

- ☐ Decision rights and escalation paths are clearly defined.
- ☐ Evidence requirements for major approvals are documented.
- ☐ Governance integrates risk management, ethics oversight, and digital asset governance.
- ☐ RACI assignments clearly identify accountable decision owners.
- ☐ Governance mechanisms have been calibrated to the project's regulatory risk, digital dependency, and societal impact.
- ☐ Governance structures enable agility while maintaining accountability.
- ☐ Transparency of decisions strengthens stakeholder trust and legitimacy.
- ☐ Reporting cadence for governance bodies is defined and understood by sponsors and project leadership.

Chapter 10
Putting It All Together

Modern projects operate in environments defined by complexity, digital traceability, regulatory pressures, and rising societal expectations.

Delivering projects on time and within budget is no longer enough.

Sustainable project success depends on disciplined integration across all performance domains.

This chapter synthesizes the principles presented throughout the book and explains how they operate as a cohesive system.

10.1 From Activities to Integrated Performance

Projects rarely fail due to a single activity being executed incorrectly.

They failed because the integration was weak.

For example:

- Scope expands without governance oversight.

- Agile delivery advances without financial control.

- AI functionality is deployed without ethical alignment.

- Data systems are implemented without accountability mapping.

Isolated excellence does not guarantee success; integration does.

Effective project leadership is not merely about managing tasks; it is about aligning different domains.

10.2 The Six Foundations of Modern Project Success

The Governance, Responsibility, Integrity, and Performance (GRIP) Framework operates through six reinforcing foundations:

1. Clear value definition
2. Structured governance
3. Agile adaptability
4. Ethical guardrails
5. Strong digital asset and record governance
6. Continuous stakeholder engagement

Each foundation strengthens the others. When one weakens, the risk increases.

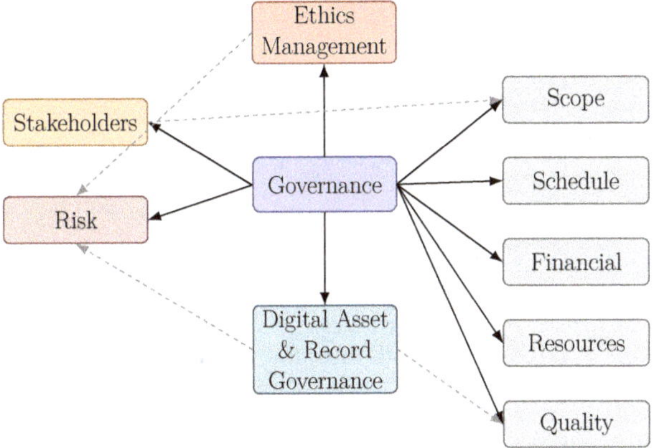

All boxes represent project management performance domains. Solid arrows indicate structural oversight. Dashed arrows indicate reinforcing integration.

Figure 10.1: Governance, Responsibility, Integrity, and Performance Framework

1. Clear Value Definition

Projects exist to create value.

The value must be:

- Explicitly defined

- Strategically aligned

- Measurable

- Defensible

Without a clear understanding of value:

- Scope becomes unstable

- Stakeholders disengage

- Governance weakens

- Ethical exposure increases

The definition of value anchors every other domain.

2. Structured Governance

Governance defines authority, escalation procedures, accountability, and oversight.

It ensures the following:

- Strategic alignment

- Financial discipline

- Risk visibility

- Ethical compliance

- Transparent decision-making

Without governance, integration will collapse.

Governance is the stabilizing core of the system.

3. Agile Adaptability

Modern environments require responsiveness.

Agile and hybrid approaches allow:

- Iterative learning

- Stakeholder feedback

- Controlled experimentation

- Progressive value realization

Adaptability must operate within established governance boundaries.

Flexibility without structure creates instability. Structure without flexibility creates stagnation.

Balance defines maturity.

4. Ethical Guardrails

Projects increasingly shape financial outcomes, access to services, employment decisions, and public trust.

Ethical guardrails ensure that value creation does not create harm.

They protect:

- Stakeholder rights

- Organizational legitimacy

- Regulatory compliance

- Long-term reputation

Responsible innovation is a form of strategic risk management.

5. Strong Digital Asset and Record Governance

Modern projects generate permanent digital records.

Decisions, approvals, models, logs, and data artifacts remain long after delivery.

Strong digital asset and record governance ensures the following:

- Traceability

- Audit readiness

- Accountability clarity

- Knowledge retention

If decisions cannot be reconstructed, accountability is weakened. If digital assets or records cannot be trusted, governance will fail.

6. Continuous Stakeholder Engagement

Stakeholders influence success before, during, and after project delivery.

Effective engagement:

- Reduces resistance

- Improves adoption

- Strengthens legitimacy

- Builds trust

Modern stakeholder analysis must consider power, legitimacy, urgency, and the potential for harm.

Engagement is continuous, not episodic.

10.3 Integration Across Domains

These six foundations operate as an integrated system.

For example:

- Governance structures shape stakeholder engagement.

- Ethical guardrails constrain value definition.

- Digital asset governance enables auditability.

- Agile adaptability requires effective financial oversight.

- Stakeholder impact influences risk-related decisions.

When domains operate independently, blind spots can emerge.

When domains are integrated, resilience improves.

Responsible project leadership exemplifies systems leadership.

Relationship to Emerging Regulatory Frameworks

The GRIP Framework closely aligns with emerging risk-based governance models, such as the EU AI Act, the NIST AI Risk Management Framework (AI RMF), and ISO/IEC 42001:2023 - Artificial Intelligence Management System. These frameworks emphasize structured oversight, defined accountability, risk-based controls, human supervision, transparency, documentation, and lifecycle monitoring.

Appendix D provides a conceptual alignment of the GRIP Framework with the EU AI Act, the NIST AI Risk Management Framework, and ISO/IEC 42001.

10.4   Leadership in the Modern Era

Modern project leaders must balance:

- Control and flexibility

- Innovation and compliance

- Speed and accountability

- Value creation and risk management

They must think beyond deliverables.

They must think in terms of:

- Long-term trust

- Governance defensibility

- Organizational sustainability

- Societal impact

Project decisions embed data, structures, and behaviors that persist long after delivery.

Leadership today is measured not only by execution but also by responsibility.

The structural mechanics of ethical oversight and digital record governance are detailed in Appendix A and Appendix B. These appendices define phase-based control structures that ensure accountability persists beyond delivery and withstands regulatory or audit scrutiny.

Final Reflection

Before approving, advancing, or closing a project, leaders should ask:

- Are we building something useful?

- Are we building it responsibly?

- Is accountability clearly defined?

- Can we explain and defend our decisions?

- Have we considered long-term consequences?

- Does this initiative strengthen trust?

- Will this project create sustainable value?

Modern project success is not defined by efficiency alone.

It is defined by responsible value creation across integrated performance domains.

Delivering results is necessary.

Leadership is demonstrated when results are achieved within clear governance, defined accountability, and ethical boundaries that preserve long-term trust.

Part IV

Closing and References

The Future of Responsible Project Leadership

Project leadership has entered a new era.

Projects today do more than deliver products and services. They shape digital ecosystems, influence human decisions, generate data at scale, and affect individuals and communities long after deployment.

In this environment, traditional measures of success—schedule and budget—are necessary but no longer sufficient.

Modern project leadership requires the integration of governance, stakeholder engagement, ethical guardrails, and structured digital asset and record management with disciplined execution.

Throughout this book, we introduced the Governance, Responsibility, Integrity, and Performance Framework as a structured response to contemporary complexity. The framework does not discard established standards. It integrates and extends them to address the realities of:

- Artificial Intelligence systems
- Cloud-based platforms

- Regulatory accountability

- Distributed stakeholder impact

- Long-term societal consequences

Projects are temporary organizations. The systems they create persist, and so does the responsibility for them.

Every decision embedded in a system, every data model trained, every governance shortcut taken, and every stakeholder ignored can reverberate far beyond the project lifecycle.

Modern project managers are not merely coordinators of tasks.

They are stewards of value.

They are architects of accountability.

They are guardians of trust.

Organizations that embrace structured governance, continuous stakeholder engagement, ethical responsibility, and disciplined digital asset and record management will not only deliver successful projects; they will create sustainable legitimacy.

Those that do not may deliver outputs, but they risk losing trust.

In a digital and AI-driven world, trust is a strategic asset.

Project leadership is no longer about controlling uncertainty alone. It is about responsibly shaping the systems that shape society.

Delivering results matters.

In the era of digital accountability, project excellence is defined not only by what is delivered, but by how responsibly it is delivered.

Appendix A: Ethics Management Performance Domain

Overview

Ethics is not a compliance add-on. It is how leaders ensure that value creation does not create harm.

Every project translates business goals into real-world impact. The Ethics Management Performance Domain ensures that this impact remains responsible, lawful, and defensible.

This domain makes ethics operational across the full project lifecycle. It defines who monitors exposure, who escalates concerns, and who answers when boundaries are crossed.

Ethics management includes:

- Clear ethics policies and governance standards

- Training to build ethical awareness and judgment

- Safe reporting channels, including whistleblower mechanisms

- Conflict-of-interest disclosure and management

- Compliance with legal, regulatory, and professional obligations

Ethical oversight is a leadership responsibility. If harm occurs, governance has failed.

The lifecycle activities by phase are shown in Table A.1.

Ethics Management Performance Domain	
Phase	**Activity**
Initiating	Align Ethics and Value
Planning	Develop Ethics Plan and Controls
Executing	Implement Ethics Safeguards
Monitoring &	Monitor Ethical Compliance
Controlling	Treat Misconduct
Closing	Conduct Ethical Review

Table A.1: Ethics Management Performance Domain Across the Project Lifecycle

Value Framework

Ethics in projects begins with understanding how value is created.

Every project operates within an economic logic, a value proposition that defines how benefits are generated and for whom. That value model may introduce risk, imbalance, or unintended impact across stakeholders.

The **value framework** provides a structured lens for examining the economic logic before lifecycle activities begin.

It:

- Makes visible how value is generated and distributed

- Identifies structural tensions or asymmetries between stakeholders

- Establishes ethical boundaries that constrain value pursuit

- Defines non-negotiable guardrails aligned with rights, law, and legitimacy

The value framework does not prescribe specific controls. It clarifies the ethical architecture within which controls must later be designed.

Appendix E provides an exemplar value framework illustrating how organizational value propositions translate into governance criteria and project-level manifestations.

Efficiency and innovation must never override responsibility.

Phase Descriptions

Initiating – Align Ethics and Value   Ethical alignment begins at initiation.

Using the value framework as a reference lens, leaders must translate ethical boundaries into explicit project commitments.

Key actions include:

- Identifying applicable laws, regulations, and professional standards

- Confirming the defined value proposition against ethical guardrails

- Assessing exposure created by the value-generation model

- Identifying affected stakeholders and rights implications

- Documenting non-negotiable ethical constraints

The outcome is a documented ethical position: What the project will pursue and what it will not compromise.

Planning – Develop Ethics Plan and Controls Ethics must be designed before pressure begins.

During planning, ethical guardrails are translated into practical controls.

This includes:

- Defining reporting and escalation pathways

- Establishing conflict-of-interest controls

- Setting up whistleblower protections

- Planning ethics training

- Defining monitoring and documentation requirements

Ethical responsibilities must be clear before execution accelerates.

Executing – Implement Ethics Safeguards   Execution is where ethical intentions are tested.

During execution, leaders must ensure that safeguards operate in practice.

This includes:

- Implementing transparency measures

- Conducting bias and fairness testing where required

- Protecting privacy and confidentiality

- Documenting sensitive decisions

- Enforcing professional standards

Ethical standards must guide daily decisions, not just formal reviews.

Monitoring & Controlling – Monitor Ethical Compliance   Leaders must actively verify that ethical commitments are being honored.

Monitoring includes:

- Internal audits and compliance reviews

- Performance and control checks

- Review of stakeholder feedback

- Verification that safeguards remain effective

If ethical controls weaken, risk increases.

Monitoring & Controlling – Treat Misconduct When misconduct occurs, a response must be immediate, structured, and accountable.

This includes:

- Investigating reported violations

- Taking corrective or disciplinary action

- Escalating significant breaches to governance authorities

- Providing redress where appropriate

- Updating controls to prevent recurrence

Ignoring misconduct undermines trust and increases exposure.

Closing – Conduct Impact Assessment Closure is not the end of responsibility.

Leaders must evaluate whether the project delivered value without causing unintended harm.

The impact assessment reviews:

- Alignment with defined ethical guardrails

- Stakeholder impact

- Regulatory obligations

- Intended and unintended consequences

Where required, the assessment aligns with formal regulatory expectations, including fundamental rights impact assessments.

Findings must be documented. Residual risks must be acknowledged. Lessons must strengthen future governance decisions.

Key Takeaways

Project leaders should confirm the following.

Leadership Checklist: Ethics Management

- [ ] The project's value proposition has been tested against ethical guardrails at initiation, before planning and delivery commitments are made.

- [ ] Applicable laws, regulations, professional standards, and rights implications have been identified.

- [ ] Non-negotiable ethical constraints are documented and understood by the project team.

- [ ] Reporting, escalation, conflict-of-interest, and whistle-blower mechanisms are defined.

- [ ] Ethics training and ethical awareness expectations are established before delivery pressure intensifies.

- [ ] Bias, fairness, privacy, confidentiality, and transparency safeguards are active during execution; sensitive decisions are documented and professional standards are enforced.

- [ ] Ethical compliance is monitored through reviews, audits, stakeholder feedback, and control checks.

- [ ] Misconduct can be investigated, escalated, corrected, redress provided where appropriate, and prevented from recurring.

- [ ] Closing includes an impact assessment of alignment with ethical guardrails, stakeholder effects, regulatory obligations including fundamental rights assessments where required, unintended harm, and residual ethical risk.

Appendix B: Digital Asset and Record Governance Performance Domain

Overview

In digital environments, every decision leaves a record. Leaders must assume that any decision may later require an explanation.

The Digital Asset and Record Governance Performance Domain ensures that records are structured, traceable, and defensible, not merely stored.

Good governance is not about collecting more documents. It is about ensuring that decisions can be reconstructed, verified, and defended.

This domain defines how information is:

- Created and classified

- Stored and protected

- Retained or disposed of

- Reviewed and disclosed when required

- Structured for future reuse

Strong digital asset and record governance supports:

- Regulatory compliance

- Audit readiness

- Organizational learning

- Long-term digital value

While digital assets may later support analytics or artificial intelligence, the primary goal of this domain is accountability, integrity, and control across the full lifecycle.

If decisions cannot be reconstructed, governance is weakened.

The lifecycle activities by phase are shown in Table B.1.

Phase Descriptions

Initiating – Define Governance Framework Digital asset and record governance must be defined before work accelerates.

At initiation, leaders must decide:

- Who owns the information

- How it will be classified

- Who can access it

- How long it must be retained

Digital Asset and Record Governance Performance Domain	
Phase	**Activity**
Initiating	Define Digital Asset and Record Governance Strategy
Planning	Plan Data Retention and Reuse
Executing	Capture Structured and Unstructured Data
Monitoring & Controlling	Monitor Data Quality and Usage
Closing	Archive
	Disclose
	Enable Reuse

Table B.1: Digital Asset and Record Governance Performance Domain Across the Project Lifecycle

- What must be disclosed under regulatory or contractual obligations

This framework ensures that information generated during the project will remain controlled, protected, and traceable.

Clear ownership at the start prevents confusion later.

Planning – Plan Retention and Reuse   Planning defines how information will be managed in practice.

Leaders must establish:

- Retention schedules and disposal rules

- Metadata standards

- Version control practices

- Storage structures

- Business continuity measures

Planning must also consider future use.

Records may later support:

- Reporting

- Audit reviews

- Regulatory disclosure

- Analytics

- Organizational learning

Information should be structured not only for todays needs but also for tomorrows accountability.

Executing – Capture and Classify Records and Assets Execution is where records are created.

Teams must systematically capture both structured and unstructured information.

Structured information may include:

- Schedules

- Cost records

- Logs and metrics

- Configuration data

Unstructured information may include:

- Communications

- Decisions and approvals

- Contracts

- Technical artifacts

Information must be classified, tagged, and stored with enough context to explain why decisions were made.

Documentation is not about volume. It is about clarity and traceability.

Monitoring & Controlling – Monitor Integrity, Access, and Usage Records must remain accurate, secure, and usable over time.

Leaders must verify:

- Completeness and accuracy

- Consistency of metadata

- Proper access authorization

- Compliance with retention policies

- Appropriate use of information

If controls weaken, exposure increases.

When gaps are identified, corrective action must follow.

Closing – Archive, Disclose, and Enable Reuse   Closure does not end responsibility for information.

At project close, records must be:

- Consolidated

- Validated

- Archived according to retention rules

Where required, disclosure packages must be prepared to meet regulatory, legal, or contractual obligations.

Archived materials should remain accessible, structured, and usable.

Well-managed records strengthen audit defensibility and support future projects.

Poorly managed records create long-term risks.

Alignment with ISO 21502 Information and Documentation Management

This performance domain aligns with ISO 21502:2020 Clause 7.16, Information and Documentation Management.

ISO 21502 emphasizes the secure and timely collection, storage, retrieval, maintenance, retention, and disposal of project information.

The Digital Asset and Record Governance Performance Domain adopts these requirements and strengthens them in three areas:

- **Lifecycle Governance:** Information control from initiation through archival and reuse.

- **Disclosure and Defensibility:** Preparing records to withstand regulatory, legal, and audit reviews.

- **Digital Asset Quality and Reuse:** Ensuring records remain reliable, traceable, and usable for analytics and organizational learning.

This domain turns documentation discipline into governance strength.

Transparency builds defensibility. Defensibility builds trust.

Key Takeaways

Project leaders should confirm the following.

Leadership Checklist: Digital Asset and Record Governance

- ☐ Information ownership, classification, access rights, retention periods, and disclosure obligations are defined at initiation.

- ☐ Retention schedules, disposal rules, metadata standards, version control, and storage structures are planned before execution accelerates.

- ☐ Both structured and unstructured records are systematically captured, classified, and stored with sufficient context.

- ☐ Record accuracy, completeness, security, and usability are actively verified through defined monitoring checks throughout the lifecycle.

- ☐ Metadata consistency, access authorization, retention compliance, and appropriate use are actively monitored.

- ☐ Corrective action is taken when record quality, integrity, or access controls weaken.

- ☐ Project closure includes validation, archiving, disclosure readiness, and preparation for future reuse.

- ☐ Documentation governance has been reviewed to confirm it meets audit, regulatory, reuse, and long-term value requirements.

- ☐ Records are structured for future reuse, including audit review, regulatory disclosure, analytics, and organisational learning, with business continuity measures defined.

Appendix C: AI Project Responsibility and Audit Framework

AI projects rarely fail because the algorithm does not work. They fail because ownership is unclear, decisions are not formally assigned, and accountability cannot be demonstrated.

In regulated or high-impact environments, unclear responsibility creates legal exposure, operational risk, and ethical vulnerability. When multiple roles assume that someone else is responsible, governance weakens, and critical decisions may go unchallenged.

This framework establishes clear, defensible accountability across the AI project lifecycle. The responsibility structure defines ownership, and the checklist verifies operational readiness.

Table C.1 defines the core responsibility areas across the AI project lifecycle and clarifies, for each area:

- The **Accountable role:** the single point of ownership who must approve the outcome and stand behind the decision.

- The **Supporting roles:** those who execute the work, provide subject-matter expertise, or must be consulted before approval.

No critical decision should proceed without an accountable owner recorded. Supporting roles contribute to analysis, implementation, or advice but do not replace ownership.

To complement the responsibility structure, the **Audit Readiness Checklist** that follows translates these ownership areas into governance control domains. It provides a practical review tool to confirm that leadership, risk, and operational controls are fully established before approval, deployment, or audit.

Used together, the responsibility structure and the checklist strengthen governance discipline, clarify decision authority, and support defensible AI delivery.

This framework operationalizes the Governance and Responsibility pillars of the GRIP Framework within AI projects.

Table C.1: AI Project Responsibility Structure

Responsibility Area	Roles and Ownership
Problem Definition and Intended Use	**Accountable:** Sponsor / Product Owner **Supporting:** Project Manager; Business Lead; Domain Experts; Legal and Compliance
Data Sourcing and Permissions	**Accountable:** Data Owner / Data Governance Lead **Supporting:** Data Engineers; Legal and Privacy; Security; Vendor
Data Quality and Bias Assessment	**Accountable:** Data Governance Lead **Supporting:** Data Scientists; Domain Experts; Quality Assurance; Ethics Lead
Model Selection and Training	**Accountable:** AI / Machine Learning Lead **Supporting:** Data Scientists; Architect; Vendor
Model Evaluation and Acceptance Criteria	**Accountable:** Sponsor / Product Owner **Supporting:** Project Manager; AI Lead; Quality Assurance; Risk; Domain Experts
Explainability and Transparency Plan	**Accountable:** Risk / Compliance Lead **Supporting:** AI Lead; Product Owner; Ethics Lead; Legal
Security Controls and Access Management	**Accountable:** Security Lead **Supporting:** Cloud / Platform Team; AI Lead; Project Manager
Human Oversight Design	**Accountable:** Business Owner / Operations Lead **Supporting:** Project Manager; Product Owner; Risk; Ethics Lead

Continued on next page

Table C.1 – continued from previous page

Responsibility Area	Roles and Ownership
Deployment Readiness and Change Control	**Accountable:** Project Manager **Supporting:** Release Manager; Operations; Vendor; Quality Assurance
Monitoring for Drift, Errors, and Harm	**Accountable:** Operations Owner **Supporting:** AI Lead; Risk; Security; Service Desk
Incident Response and Accountability Actions	**Accountable:** Operations Owner / Sponsor **Supporting:** Project Manager; Legal; Risk; Security; Communications
Ethical Review and Stakeholder Impact	**Accountable:** Ethics Lead (or Governance Board) **Supporting:** Sponsor; Project Manager; Domain Experts; Legal and Privacy
Audit Trail and Retention (End-to-End)	**Accountable:** Digital Asset and Record Governance Lead **Supporting:** Project Manager; Project Management Office; Security; AI Lead

Action step: Review and formally reapprove this structure at each major project checkpoint (initiation, design approval, go-live, and post-deployment review).

Table C.2: Audit Readiness Checklist (Governance)

Confirm that each governance domain is complete before approval, go-live, or audit.

1. Purpose and Accountability (Sponsor / Product Owner)

☐ Business case clearly approved.

☐ Intended use and system boundaries documented.

☐ Success measures defined.

☐ Accountable owner formally assigned and recorded.

2. Data and Model Integrity (Data Governance Lead / AI Lead)

☐ Legal basis for data use documented.

☐ Data inventory and quality assessment completed.

☐ Bias assessment performed and remediation actions logged.

☐ Model rationale, training records, and validation evidence retained.

Table C.3: Audit Readiness Checklist (Operational Control)

---

3. Risk, Security and Compliance (Risk / Compliance / Security Leads)

☐ Explainability and transparency approach documented.

☐ System limitations and risks identified.

☐ Security controls implemented and tested.

☐ Regulatory and policy alignment reviewed.

4. Operations and Lifecycle Control (Operations Owner / Project Manager)

☐ Human oversight and escalation processes defined.

☐ Deployment approvals and change controls recorded.

☐ Monitoring and drift detection active.

☐ Incident response and audit trail documentation maintained.

If any domain cannot be confirmed, approval or deployment should be formally withheld.

Appendix D: Conceptual Alignment of the GRIP Framework, NIST AI RMF, and the EU AI Act

The GRIP Framework closely aligns with emerging risk-based governance models, such as the European Union AI Act, the NIST AI Risk Management Framework (AI RMF), and ISO/IEC 42001:2023 - Artificial Intelligence Management System. These frameworks emphasize structured oversight, defined accountability, risk-based controls, human supervision, transparency, documentation, and lifecycle monitoring. While the EU AI Act establishes binding regulatory obligations, the NIST AI RMF provides voluntary risk management guidance, and ISO/IEC 42001 introduces a certifiable management system structure, all three reinforce the need for systematic governance of AI systems.

While regulatory requirements will continue to evolve across jurisdictions, the underlying governance principles remain stable. Clear decision rights, documented oversight, traceable records, defensible risk management, and continuous improvement are not temporary compliance trends; they are essential structural elements.

Organizations that embed governance architecture rather than react to compliance mandates build resilience against regulatory uncertainty. The GRIP Framework provides this structural foundation by operationalizing governance, responsibility, integrity, and performance as an integrated lifecycle system. This system is capable of adapting to new legal requirements and evolving management system expectations while preserving trust, defensibility, and long-term value.

Table D.1: GRIP, NIST AI RMF, EU AI Act, and ISO/IEC 42001 Conceptual Alignment

Dimension	Alignment Across Frameworks
Structured Governance	**GRIP:** Decision rights, escalation, lifecycle accountability. **NIST AI RMF:** GOVERN function establishes roles, responsibilities, and risk tolerance. **EU AI Act:** Requires risk management systems, technical documentation, and supervisory oversight for high-risk AI. **ISO/IEC 42001:** Establishes an AI Management System (AIMS) with defined leadership accountability and governance controls.

Continued on next page

Table D.1 – continued from previous page

Dimension	Alignment Across Frameworks
Risk-Based Controls	**GRIP:** Risk thresholds and proportional governance intensity. **NIST AI RMF:** MAPMEASUREMANAGE functions structure AI risk identification, analysis, and mitigation. **EU AI Act:** Tiered regulatory obligations based on system risk classification. **ISO/IEC 42001:** Formal risk assessment and treatment processes embedded within the management system.
Human Accountability	**GRIP:** Accountability is non-transferable; autonomy increases oversight requirements. **NIST AI RMF:** Emphasizes defined human roles, oversight processes, and documentation. **EU AI Act:** Mandates human oversight by competent natural persons; deployers retain responsibility. **ISO/IEC 42001:** Requires the assignment of roles, competence assurance, and accountability within the AI management system.
Transparency & Traceability	**GRIP:** Lifecycle traceability, defensible documentation, and digital asset governance. **NIST AI RMF:** Encourages explainability, interpretability, and contextual documentation. **EU AI Act:** Logging, technical documentation, and transparency obligations for high-risk systems. **ISO/IEC 42001:** Requires documented information control, monitoring, logging, and audit evidence retention.

Continued on next page

Table D.1 – continued from previous page

Dimension	Alignment Across Frameworks
Ethics & Fundamental Rights	**GRIP:** Ethical guardrails and structured stakeholder protection mechanisms. **NIST AI RMF:** Trustworthiness characteristics include fairness, bias mitigation, and socio-technical awareness. **EU AI Act:** Explicit protection of fundamental rights and bias mitigation requirements. **ISO/IEC 42001:** Requires consideration of societal impact, fairness, and responsible AI objectives within governance processes.
Lifecycle Orientation	**GRIP:** Integrated governance from initiation through post-deployment review. **NIST AI RMF:** Continuous lifecycle risk management across design, development, deployment, and monitoring. **EU AI Act:** Pre-market conformity assessment and post-market monitoring obligations. **ISO/IEC 42001:** Operates under a Plan-Do-Check-Act (PDCA) continuous improvement lifecycle model.
System Certification Structure	**GRIP:** Not a certifiable standard; provides governance and leadership framework guidance. **NIST AI RMF:** Voluntary risk management framework; not a certification regime. **EU AI Act:** Regulatory conformity assessment is required for high-risk systems; market surveillance enforcement is mandated. **ISO/IEC 42001:** Certifiable international AI Management System standard (AIMS).

Appendix E: Exemplar Value Framework

Overview

Every organization defines a value proposition that drives its economic logic.

For example, insurance companies reduce costs by monetizing risk through data, AI, and predictive models. To do this, they seek consumer data that improves their ability to rate individual risk levels. Consumers may benefit from more personalized pricing. However, they may also have concerns about consent, privacy, and discrimination.

Another example is usage-based insurance that uses the global positioning system and speedometer data to rate a persons driving behavior. The insurer benefits from more accurate pricing. The customer may benefit from lower premiums. At the same time, questions arise about data usage, fairness, and transparency.

Similarly, machine manufacturers increasingly collect usage patterns from built-in sensors on their equipment. The manufacturer benefits from insights that improve design, enable new services, or reduce costs. Machine owners may benefit from greater efficiency and productivity. However, they may not fully understand how the data is used or how it could influence usage terms, pricing, or future service conditions.

In each case, value is created, but it is not distributed equally across stakeholders.

The Exemplar Value Framework[2] illustrates how an organizations value proposition flows into responsible value creation, stakeholder impact, governance criteria, and concrete project actions. It bridges economic logic with structured governance design.

The framework does not remove value imbalance. It ensures that trade-offs are consciously designed, transparently governed, and defensible over time. Figure E.1 provides a process for the value framework, and Table E.1 provides an illustrative example using an insurance case.

Governance Criteria

Value creation must be assessed against defined criteria:

- Purpose limitation

- Lawful and transparent data usage

- Individual access and rectification rights

- Proportionality of data collection

- Bias detection and mitigation

- Documented accountability

These criteria convert ethical exposure into auditable governance controls.

Project-Level Manifestations

Governance criteria only become meaningful when translated into tangible project artifacts. In practice, this includes:

- Data classification and retention controls

- Algorithm validation reports

- Consent capture mechanisms

- Impact assessments

- Stakeholder review gates

- Post-deployment monitoring triggers

Without manifestation in artifacts, governance remains theoretical.

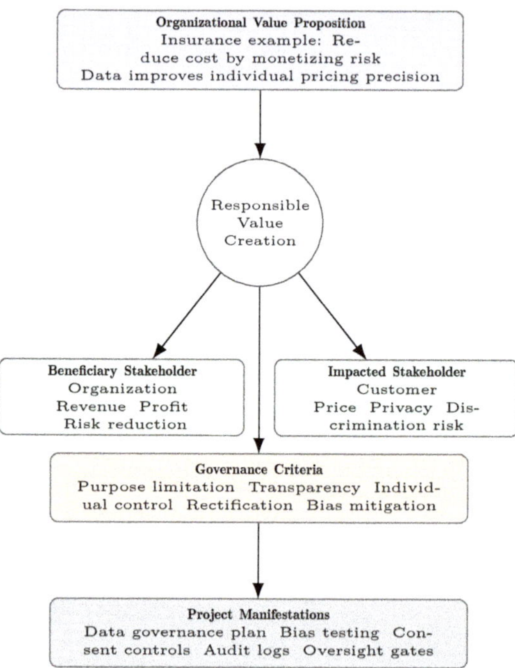

Figure E.1: Exemplar Value Framework

Table E.1: Operationalizing the Exemplar Value Framework (A6 Layout)

Value Proposition	Governance Criteria	Project Manifestation
Element: Target Value		
Reduce loss ratio through data-driven risk pricing	Purpose clarity; proportionality; transparent rationale	Approved business case; defined scope; intended-use statement
Element: Beneficiary Stakeholder (Organization)		
Revenue/Profit: Improve pricing precision; grow profitable segments	Pricing accountability; auditability; approval gates	Governance review; model acceptance criteria; decision logs
Risk control: Detect fraud; reduce claims leakage	False-positive thresholds; due process; escalation triggers	Monitoring dashboards; incident playbook; review workflow
Element: Impacted Stakeholder (Customer)		
Price/Access: Enable personalized premiums	Non-discrimination; representativeness; explainability	Bias testing; fairness metrics; explanation summary
Privacy: Protect personal data	Consent validity; data minimization; retention limits	Consent records; retention schedule; impact assessment (if required)
Contestability: Challenge adverse outcomes	Right to review; rectification; human override	Appeals process; human review queue; correction mechanism
Element: Data Governance (System Enabler)		
Acquire and use data to improve model accuracy	Lawful basis; provenance; licensing; surveillance limits	Data inventory; lineage logs; vendor register

Continued on next page

Value Proposition	Governance Criteria	Project Manifestation
Element: Model Governance (System Enabler)		
Automate underwriting decisions efficiently	Robustness; drift monitoring; change control	Model cards; version control; drift dashboard; release approvals
Element: Lifecycle Accountability and Value Realization		
Sustain value through ongoing monitoring	Periodic review; accountability persistence	Post-deployment reviews; KPI tracking; audit pack

End Notes

[1] These findings are based on an extended version of research conducted between 2023 and 2025 on accountability in artificial intelligence projects (Miller, 2025b). The findings are based on quantitative analysis of survey data from more than 300 respondents across the United States, Germany, China, and South Africa.

[2] Adapted from value co-creation theory (Breidbach & Maglio, 2020) and AI governance operationalization research (Yurrita et al., 2022).

Bibliography

Association for Project Management. (2019). APM body of knowledge 7th edition.

Breidbach, C. F., & Maglio, P. (2020). Accountable algorithms? the ethical implications of data-driven business models. *Journal of Service Management, 31*(2), 163–185. https://doi.org/10.1108/JOSM-03-2019-0073

European Union. (2024). Regulation (EU) 2024/1689 of the european parliament and of the council of 13 june 2024 laying down harmonised rules on artificial intelligence and amending regulations (EC) no 300/2008, (EU) no 167/2013, (EU) no 168/2013, (EU) 2018/858, (EU) 2018/1139 and (EU) 2019/2144 and directives 2014/90/eu, (EU) 2016/797 and (EU) 2020/1828 (Artificial Intelligence Act).

International Standards Organization. (2020). ISO 21502: 2020-12 project, programme and portfolio management guidance on project management first edition.

International Standards Organization. (2023). ISO/IEC 42001: 2023-12 information technology artificial intelligence management system first edition.

Miller, G. J. (2022). Stakeholder roles in artificial intelligence projects. *Project Leadership Society, 3, Art. no. 100068*. https://doi.org/10.1016/j.plas.2022.100068

Miller, G. J. (2025a). *Framework for managing artificial intelligence (AI) projects: Avoiding harms, losses, and damages* (K. D. Strang & N. R. Vajjhala, Eds.). Springer Nature Switzerland. https://doi.org/10.1007/978-3-031-80275-1_7

Miller, G. J. (2025b). Simultaneous pursuit of accountability for regulatory compliance, financial benefits, and societal impacts in artificial intelligence (ai) projects. *2025 20th Conference on Computer Science and Intelligence Systems (FedCSIS)*, 207–217. https://doi.org/10.15439/2025F6392

Mitchell, R. K., Agle, B. R., & Wood, D. J. (1997). Toward a theory of stakeholder identification and salience: Defining the principle of who and what really counts. *Academy of Management Review, 22*(4), 853–886. https://doi.org/10.5465/amr.1997.9711022105

Project Management Institute. (2025). Pmbok guide: A guide to the project management body of knowledge - Eighth edition.

Tabassi, E. (2023, January). Artificial intelligence risk management framework (AI RMF 1.0). https://doi.org/10.6028/NIST.AI.100-1

The Stationery Office. (2017). Managing successful projects with Prince2.

Yurrita, M., Murray-Rust, D., Balayn, A., & Bozzon, A. (2022). Towards a multi-stakeholder value-based assessment framework for algorithmic systems. https: //doi.org/10.1145/3531146.3533118

Glossary

accountability The obligation of a person or role to answer for decisions, outcomes, and impacts; accountability cannot be delegated to an automated system.

algorithm A step-by-step set of instructions that a computer follows to process data and produce a result or decision.

artificial intelligence (AI) Computer systems designed to perform tasks that normally require human intelligence, such as learning, reasoning, or decision-making.

audit readiness The state in which decisions, controls, evidence, and records are sufficiently complete and traceable to withstand internal or external review.

automation–autonomy continuum A conceptual scale describing how much a system automates tasks versus acts with goal-directed autonomy; higher autonomy requires stronger oversight and controls.

benefits realization The discipline of defining, tracking, and achieving measurable outcomes from a project, beyond producing deliverables.

bias Systematic unfairness in data, models, decisions, or outcomes that disadvantages certain individuals or groups.

change control A governance process for evaluating, approving, implementing, and recording changes to scope, requirements, configuration, or operating controls.

cloud governance Policies and controls for cost, security, access, architecture, and operational responsibility within cloud-based delivery environments.

controls Defined mechanisms (preventive, detective, corrective) that reduce risk, enforce policy, and enable defensible operation and oversight.

data quality Fitness of data for its intended use, including accuracy, completeness, timeliness, consistency, and representativeness.

data subject An individual whose personal data is processed; the data subject holds specific rights regarding that processing.

decision log A structured record of key decisions, rationale, evidence, approvers, and dates to support traceability and defensibility.

defensibility The ability to justify decisions and outcomes using documented rationale, evidence, controls, and appropriate governance.

diffusion of responsibility A failure mode where many roles contribute to outcomes but no single role clearly owns the decision, leading to weak governance and accountability gaps.

digital asset and record governance Policies and processes for record keeping, retention, access control, audit trail integrity, and reuse of project and operational artifacts.

ethics management Structured practices that ensure projects align value creation with ethical principles, protect rights, prevent harm, and address misconduct.

European Union Artificial Intelligence Act (EU AI Act) A binding European Union regulation establishing a risk-based legal framework for Artificial Intelligence systems.

GOVERN–MAP–MEASURE–MANAGE Core functional structure of the NIST AI Risk Management Framework.

governance The system of authority, decision rights, oversight, escalation, and accountability that directs and controls a project or program.

harm Negative impact on individuals, groups, or society, including unfair treatment, privacy violations, loss of opportunity, or safety risks.

harm potential The likelihood and severity of negative impact on a stakeholder group, especially important for low-power but highly affected stakeholders.

human oversight The design and operational practice of ensuring humans can review, intervene, override, and remain accountable for system outcomes.

intended use The specific purpose and context for which a system is designed, approved, and deployed; essential for managing ethical and regulatory exposure.

International Electrotechnical Commission An international standards organization that develops and publishes global standards for electrical, electronic, and related technologies. In the context of AI governance, IEC collaborates with ISO to develop joint standards such as ISO/IEC 42001 for Artificial Intelligence management systems.

International Organization for Standardization (ISO) An independent international body that develops globally recognized voluntary standards. ISO standards support consistent practices in areas such as project management, quality management, information governance, and artificial intelligence management systems.

misconduct Violation of defined ethical, legal, or governance standards; requires detection, escalation, investigation, and corrective action.

model drift A change over time in model performance or behavior due to shifting data, context, user behavior, or system interactions.

NIST AI Risk Management Framework (NIST AI RMF) A voluntary framework published by the U.S. National Institute of Standards and Technology (NIST) that provides structured guidance for identifying, assessing, managing, and governing risks associated with Artificial Intelligence systems.

oversight Active monitoring and review by accountable roles or governance bodies to ensure controls operate and decisions remain aligned to intent.

risk threshold A predefined trigger level at which escalation, mitigation, stopping, or scaling decisions must be considered.

stakeholder Any individual, group, or organization that can influence a project or is affected by its outcomes; stakeholders are defined by impact, not by contract.

traceability The ability to link decisions, data, requirements, controls, and outcomes through documented evidence across the lifecycle.

transparency The degree to which decisions, limitations, risks, and operating practices are explainable, visible, and documented for appropriate audiences.

Acronyms

AI Artificial Intelligence.

APM Association for Project Management.

CD Continuous Delivery.

CI Continuous Integration.

EU European Union.

GenAI Generative Artificial Intelligence.

GRIP Governance, Responsibility, Integrity, and Performance Framework.

IEC International Electrotechnical Commission.

ISO International Organization for Standardization.

ML Machine Learning.

NIST National Institute of Standards and Technology.

NLP Natural Language Processing.

PMBOK Project Management Body of Knowledge.

RACI Responsible, Accountable, Consulted, Informed.

RMF Risk Management Framework.

SLA Service Level Agreement.

Index

www.ingramcontent.com/pod-product-compliance
Lightning Source LLC
Chambersburg PA
CBHW041318120726
48005CB00014B/2041